Hydroponics For Beginners

The Beginner's Guide to Building a Sustainable and Inexpensive Hydroponic System at Home: Learn How to Quickly Start Growing Plants in Water

Abel Parr

Furthermore, the information that can be found within the pages described forthwith shall be considered both accurate and truthful when it comes to the recounting of facts. As such, any use, correct or incorrect, of the provided information will render the Publisher free of responsibility as to the actions taken outside of their direct purview. Regardless, there are zero scenarios where the original author or the Publisher can be deemed liable in any fashion for any damages or hardships that may result from any of the information discussed herein.

Additionally, the information in the following pages is intended only for informational purposes and should thus be thought of as universal. As befitting its nature, it is presented without assurance regarding its prolonged validity or interim quality. Trademarks that are mentioned are done without written consent and can in no way be considered an endorsement from the trademark holder.

INTRODUCTION

Hydroponics is on the rise, putting its global valuation at about $21.4 billion in 2015. Great global developments are on the horizon which is expected to intensify the development of this form of farming.

Out of necessity these reforms will be made to meet a rapidly expanding global population. We are already using a large proportion of the land available to produce crops, and new farming methods need to be created to increase yields or make other land viable for crop production. Vertical urban farming is a prospective farming approach that solves the problem of inadequate land, and works with hydroponics really well.

Hydroponics is the process of growing soil-less plants by delivering a steady solution of nutrients to them. Although this approach remains fairly unfamiliar outside of a small sector of the horticultural community, it has been around for a long time in fact. It is a device that has been commonly used in Babylon's hanging gardens, and has been extensively studied for the past few hundred years by scientists and horticulturalists.

There are many important explanations for commercial food producers to use this approach but the domestic gardener able to produce a high yield in a limited amount of space is also using it more often today. Although this is used mainly as a way to produce crops for the table, it is also a tool that can be used for ornamental plant growth.

All plants require nutrients from soil, light and dissolved to expand. Hydroponics allows for the delivery of a very specifically regulated quantity of nutrients, dissolved in water, directly to the root system as needed by the plant. Because the root system is no longer required to stretch so far to obtain the nutrients, this in turn allows the grower to plant his crops at much higher densities, and that's just another reason why hydroponic crop yields are that much higher than typical soil yields.

There are a variety of variants on the hydroponic theme, and there are plenty of options available to gardeners. Although some of the approaches may seem too complex for the home gardener, I urge you to continue because in many situations what may seem to be a difficult scheme to replicate at first is in fact surprisingly easy and the rise in yields will be astounding.

CHAPTER 1

About hydroponics

Primitive forms of hydroponics have been practiced for thousands of years by different societies. The term hy droponic itself derives from a fusion of two words from Ancient Greek, hydro for water and ponic for job. In other words, when he started to pursue agriculture, the water was meant to do the job that had produced such toil for mankind.

Different forms of it have been carried on in Cashmere for centuries, and one group, the American Aztecs, has developed a form of floating garden. Pushed by other more hostile groups into the marshy areas of Lake Tenochtitlan in what is now Mexico, these nomadic people were forced to come up with a viable agricultural system to survive. They created a network of floating rafts woven together from reeds that gradually transformed in to a floating island archipelago. Such islands were teeming with herbs, flowers and even fruit. The historian William Prescott recorded the colonizing Spaniards ' conquest of the Aztec empire and identified the floating gardens as' Wondering islands of Verdure, teeming with flowers and vegetables and rolling on the water like rafts.' Some historians believe that hydroponics was an important ingredient in the development of Babylon's famed hanging gardens, which was one of the seventeen. If that is the case, then this is potentially the first example of the hydroponics used as a form of farming.

The first scientific studies took place in more modern times in the 1600s, when the Belgian Jan van Helmont demonstrated that you could cultivate a willow in a tube containing 200 pounds of dry soil and feeding only with rain water. The willow shoot had achieved a weight of 160 pounds after five years while the soil had only shrunk by two ounces in weight. He concluded that plants are getting what they need from water for production. Although partially correct in his observations, the need for carbon dioxide and oxygen, which are also critical for plant growth, was not taken into account by early demonstration.

John Woodwards took the method a further stage in 1699 when he produced plants in water containing differing amounts of contaminated soil. The plants which had the highest soil concentrations grew fastest. In this early version of the man-made hydroponic solution Woodwards realized that soil probably contained some nutrient crucial to plant growth but he was unable to identify what those nutrients were with chemistry yet to be discovered.

In the decades that followed, research began to gather momentum and scientists were able to prove that plants consumed water from their roots, and that this then progressed into their structures to be released by pores in the leaves. We also noticed the roots extracting nitrogen and oxygen and leaves taking carbon dioxide from the soil as well.

In 1851, French chemist Jean Baptist Boussingault began experimenting with inert rising media and water with different combinations of soil-based materials. In 1860 Professor Julius von Sachs released the first nutrient solution in which plants can be grown. Different solutions continued to be developed but all experiments had been focused on laboratory work at this point. It was not until the 1920's that Doctor William Gericke started to expand lab work to include agricultural crop production. He justified the use of the term hydroponics in the process and laid the groundwork as we know it for all forms of modern hydroponics. Developments have persisted, of course, and this is still an emerging science today, but we now have a much better handle on growing plant methods without using soil.

There are several major benefits to using this approach to grow plants. We eliminate pests and diseases borne by the soil right away. Greater control over the plants makes scale and output more predictable. Since the water is reused, water wastes are massively reduced. Crops mature faster often allowing for two crops per year where only one can be produced in conventional soil growing systems and eventually greater yields. It is almost certain in a world of diminishing natural resources and rapidly increasing population growth that this will be a field of agricultural production that sees massive growth.

Gericke had proven that the plants needed no soil, it was the nutrients and moisture that the soil contained along with adequate support for the plants. This could be provided just as, and possibly even more effectively, by adding to the water the exact nutrient requirements and then growing the plant purely for stability and support in an inert mean. Nutrients continue to be leached out from the plant roots in the soil, thereby causing the plant to stretch the root system continually in an effort to reach them. Nutrients can be substituted but in an environment where the leaching can not be monitored or assessed precisely, it is difficult to estimate the exact requirements that a plant requires. This creates a further disadvantage in that the plant must waste valuable energy in the production of root crops that could be diverted to crops. The root system produces nutrients while developing in soil, which serves as an anchor and shelter for the plant. Provided that the plant is given plenty of nutrients then the root system can be considerably smaller and the anchorage function in any non-leaching material can take place. Many hydroponic systems completely eliminate the planting medium and suspend the vine, feeding the trailing roots through a nebula. This approach is effective to perfection.

The initial structures of Gericke quickly proved too advanced for most would be hydroponic farmers. One of the main problems was to maintain a consistent oxygen supply in the solution to the nutrients. Concern in the methods he developed had been sparked, however, and since then continuing advances have made hydroponics more and more basic. Now over the planet there are huge green house farmers generating very high yields. There are now more than 1.000. 000 soilless household units in the United States. Some figures show the need to establish this system: 3.7 million acres of land were developed in 1950, and a population of just under 151 000 000 inhabitants. Today that population has risen to 204 000 000, and the amount of land under cultivation has fallen to 3.2 million acres. With numbers like this it is clear that there is a rise in the need for productive crop production and it is possible that less soil will be available for it to flourish on.

Roof tops are one region that is constantly being looked at and used. Vast flat surfaces within the boundaries of towns provide a great place to grow crops. What's more, as we start producing crops in urban environments we significantly reduce the amount of miles that the crops have to migrate to get to the end user with a knock back effects, both in terms of emissions generated and end product freshness.

Nonetheless, modern hydroponics can go even smaller. Nowadays it's easy for a homeowner to set up his own hydroponic garden in the backyard and there are even smaller kitchen and apartment units designed. In these situations, the principal water and electricity requirements are already in place. This is what you'll need to make your own machine at its most basic level.

A chamber rising, or a tray. This will include the growth medium and plant roots, and can be anything that holds water and is big enough for the plants that you want to grow.

A cistern. This will include the water and nutrient network which will then be injected in cyclical motion to the expanding chamber. Again it can be made from just about anything as long as it holds sufficiently material. However, it should be light proof to inhibit the algae and microorganism growth.

A pump which is submersible. This does not have to be expensive, and pumps water back and forth from the reservoir to the growing chamber. Pumps from fish ponds are commonly used.

Any distribution system. This is only a method for moving the solution from the tank to the container. The PVC tubing works just fine.

You already have a simple but working framework on which to base. One addition is a timer that would make your life easier and cost very little. This will turn the pump on and off and guarantee that the plant roots are kept moist at all times. An air pump, even as basic as you can see in small fish ponds, can help to keep the water oxygenated that is necessary for plant growth and will also allow proper distribution of the nutrients. The air pump is normally located inside the reservoir. Remember that the roots must be kept in the dark to perform at their best so it may be necessary to cover them in some way depending on what growing medium you use.

Growing lights are another addition that will give you greater control and increase the optimum period of growth, but in the most basic units they are not necessary. You may want to find an additional timer for those if you opt for rising lights.

You can make this very simple system at home or you can buy it as a premade kit. There are even examples of people making a machine by stringing plastic soda bottles across an apartment window and connecting them with PVC tubing and swirling the nutrient solution around with very good results.

The point I am trying to say is that this plant processing system is no longer restricted to specialist teams on large scale only. There is little use in growing your own tomatoes if the start-up costs are such that you owe twenty dollars to every tomato you make.

BENEFITS OF HYDROPHONICS

Hydroponics is a method for growing soilless plants, using only water, a nutrient solution, and a structure for keeping the plants up. While diverse aspects of water culture have been practiced for several thousand years, the science behind hydroponics has been more fully understood only in the last 100 years.

This has helped both domestic and commercial growers to grow plants in new ways with specific advantages and disadvantages.

Here is everything about the positive aspects of hydroponics that have certainly contributed to the rapidly increasing hydroponic cultivation industry.

Hydroponics is part of a broader push to increase agricultural productivity, yield and lower food production costs. Close behind this, domestic hydroponics grew, with a growing number of enthusiasts growing all kinds of plants at home.

BETTER SPACE MANAGEMENT

Hydroponically growing plants need 20 percent less water than plants grown in soil. It means you can grow more plants in a given area, or grow plants in very small spaces where soil-based plants would not be feasible.

This has drastic consequences for the agricultural industry, where many plants are cultivated in costly indoor greenhouses, where optimal use of space is key to producing a decent return on the investment.

The main reason for this is that hydroponic plants require less space than plants grown in the soil, and the roots do not need to disperse in the soil to look for nutrients and water. Depending on the particular hydroponic process, water and nutrients are delivered directly to the roots, either intermittently or continuously. As a consequence, the roots are more compact, and may grow closer together. Because less space is needed, farmers, with less resources, may produce significantly higher yields.

NO SOIL NEED

For Hydroponics: The notion of growing soil-free produce was once a foreign concept but is now a reality for domestic and commercial production.

Growing soilless plants have a number of benefits.

Soil quality varies widely from one place to the next and many plants have strong preferences for a particular type of soil. If you do not have this type of soil available, importation of suitable soil or alteration of your current soil can be costly and labor intensive.

There are even a variety of places around the globe that don't have access to the surface, or where land is limited. One of the first commercial hydroponic farming projects in the Pacific region was on Wake Island. This is a rocky atoll which has no good soil for plant growth.

This island was used as a Pan American Airlines refueling station during the 1930s. Importing fresh produce would have been prohibitively expensive so hydroponics was used efficiently to expand the supplies needed.

Certain countries with little arable land, including desert or mountainous areas, would no longer be restricted by how much they can expand. This is a motivating factor for a hydroponic change, which is essentially why future cultivation is considered. In these areas the production opportunities are greatly increased. These can reduce the need to import fresh produce, and can reduce water use, which in many countries can also be a concern.

HYDROPONICS SAVES WATER

Hydroponic Plants will thrive with just 5-10% of the water needed for soil growth. This is of enormous benefit in regions where water resources are scarce, and is a major environmental advantage to hydroponic farming.

Hydroponics capitalizes on recirculated soil, where plants consume what they need, collecting the run-off and adding it to the network. The only water that is lost is through leakage and evaporation, but if necessary a successful system will mitigate both.

Many hydroponic systems make much better use of technologies to further reduce water pollution. The truth is, 95 per cent of all the water plants draw in through their roots is absorbed into the soil.

As a result, some industrial hydroponic devices use condensers of water vapor to recapture this water and return it to the system.

Global food demand keeps growing year after year, and uses more water than ever before. We are endangering our planet's ecosystem unless we use technology such as hydroponics to allow more sustainable agriculture.

CLIMATE CONTROL

Hydroponic ecosystems give total climate control. Temperature, light intensity and duration and even air quality can be modified, all according to what is required for optimum production. It provides an outlet for exporting whatever the season, so producers can increase productivity throughout the year, and customers can buy goods however they want.

PLANTS GROW FASTER AND BIGGER WITH HYDROPONICS

What is interesting with hydroponics is the growth efficiency. One would think hydroponics would result in lower yields but the opposite is true. There is room for faster growth than with soil, enabled by the ability to control temperature, humidity, light and nutrients.

Ideal environments are created to ensure plants obtain the right amount of nutrients that come into direct contact with roots. Therefore plants do not need to waste valuable energy seeking contaminated nutrients in the soil. Instead, they should turn their attention to growing and producing fruit, leading to a better growth rate and larger plants.

MORE CONTROL OVER PH

PH levels are sometimes ignored by farmers, but it is a crucial aspect of cultivation that guarantees that your plants can obtain sufficient amounts of the nutrients they need to grow healthily.

Unlike growing plants in soil, the growing solution completely contains essential minerals for growth. The pH of this solution can be easily adjusted and accurately measured to maintain an ideal pH at all times.

Ensuring optimal pH increases the potential of a plant to take up essential minerals. If the PH levels change too much, plants may lack nutrient absorption capabilities. While some plants flourish in slightly acidic growth conditions, the pH levels will usually vary from 5.5 -7. Growers would be prudent to explore optimum PH levels for the plant in question, and understand how hydroponic growth makes effective regulation possible.

Any pests, plagues, or fungus weeds are time-consuming to eradicate from the soil and can have an effect on the growth of the plants you cultivate. These are no longer a problem with hydroponics. Soil-borne rodents are likewise no concern.

Most hydroponic growing systems do not require pesticides as a consequence of the soil-free environment, which can make the plant safer for human consumption and avoid the complications that pesticides can create for the climate. In a closed hydroponic culture environment you can take control of local variables more quickly.

HYDROPONICS IS LESS LABOR INTENSIVE

Although the construction costs of a hydroponic system are certainly more costly, whether for domestic or industrial use, the labor involved in plant production are significantly reduced. It frees up the time to concentrate on other tasks, instead of tilling, hoeing, plowing, etc. The running costs may also be reduced over time, although this varies on the system in question.

CLIMATE IS NOT A CONCERN

Whether you use a small hydroponic device to grow a few tomatoes on your windowsill, or you operate a commercial hydroponic far away, you will eradicate a major cause of plant growth instability. Since most hydroponic plants are grown either indoors or in greenhouses and all necessary water and nutrients are supplied manually, you remove the confusion that comes with unpredictable weather conditions.

Even sunshine need not be a problem, as artificial rising lighting will substitute or complement sunlight. Using artificial growing lights can let you grow plants throughout the year. Actually I use LED growth lights to help me grow tomatoes and salad greens throughout the whole year. The fresh salad is hard to beat whenever you need it.

HYDROPONICS IS A WONDERFUL HOBBY

A number of years ago I developed an interest in hydroponics as a hobby and I absolutely love it. Using hydroponics you can start growing plants at very little upfront cost. You can use lots of DIY and pre-built solutions and this is really modular.

You can continue your windowsill by growing only one or two plants. That's how I started and made me learning a lot about what plants need to grow and thrive. From there, you can ramp things up and there's really no limit to how far you can take the hobby.

Though I also like outdoor gardens, I love having greenery in my house and growing vegetables and salad greens throughout the year is so rewarding that I can use it to feed my family.

CHAPTER 2

The Different Hydroponic Systems

Although in fact there is a lot of variety in the different types of hydroponic systems it is limited to six different types. The drip system, the ebb and flow system, N.F.T., the water science system, aeroponics and the wick system. These devices can all be adjusted to suit the individual user's atmosphere and budget, and the space they have available. If selecting a suitable program for your own needs you need to consider these things as well as the size and form of plant you are going to grow. Do note that from time to time, units will need to be washed very carefully so that you can quickly disassemble and clean a device.

THE DRIP SYSTEM

This is one of the most common systems for both home gardener and company maker. One of the main reasons it's so common is that it's promoting large plant growth. Every plant is essentially potted into a growing medium in a single pot. A drip line is then applied to each pot from the tank, and when the pump is turned on a nutrient solution drips into the pots until the medium is soaked through.

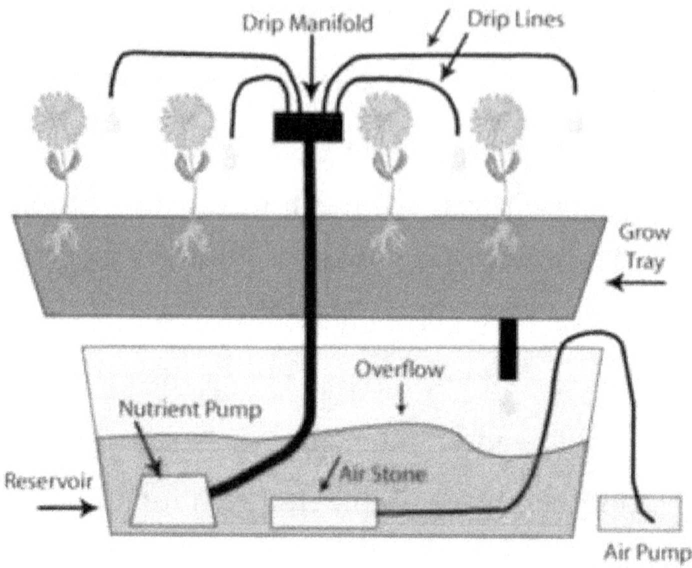

The excess solution then drains through the pot to where it is collected by means of gravity in a tray which returns it to the reservoir. Just before the medium gets dry, the timer is set to turn the pump on again, so the roots are kept constantly moist.

Such systems tend to circulate in domestic units but some exchange units are non-circulating. That occurs in these greater operations is that it is not detected when the water drains through the growing medium. This may seem inefficient but it depends on the fact that the timer is so precise that it gives the rising medium enough solution to wet it perfectly with very little waste when set correctly. It then applies additional water just before the product dries out.

The industrial grower has doubled the profit. Firstly, he is not expected to have a huge area of catchment trays carrying the solution back to the reservoir and, secondly, each time he tops up the reservoir, he will add the exact amount of nutrient that matches the needs of the plants. The nutrients within a system decrease as they are consumed by the plant and thus a circulation system must be periodically tested to determine the levels of nutrients.

The tank must be updated regularly in a non-circulating environment, but in large-scale projects there are usually personnel in place to ensure so.

EBB AND FLOW SYSTEM

This is a solution that fits the domestic user's smaller scale either in the house or in the garden because it is easy to build and can be designed to fit into any space available. Plants are potted into a rising medium and put in a rather deep tray. At a depth of one or two inches below the rising medium surface, an overflow line is attached to the tray and water is then pumped into the tray from the reservoir.

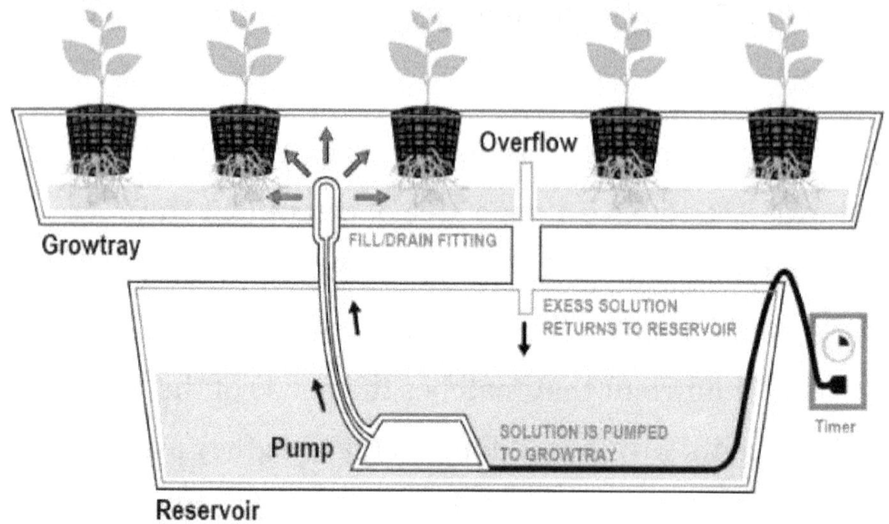

When the level of water hits the excess it just runs back to the reservoir. When a float valve opens this turns the engine off, when the tank refills the same valve turns the water back on again. In this way the plant's roots are continually sunk into water and removed again. It is a device that can be built on a very small scale and this process is used by many pre-made devices. Make sure that the overflow pipe is large enough to carry water faster than it can reach via the pump while constructing your own network.

TECHNIQUE OF NUTRIENT FILM

In this method plants are grown in a matt medium like rock wool and put in a tray with a fine film at its foundation. A pump takes through the film the nutrients and this soaks the film leaving the roots continuously moist. Excess water simply runs by gravity back into the reservoir. Typically, plants are planted through some kind of substrate to deter light from entering the roots as there is no growing surface to protect them.

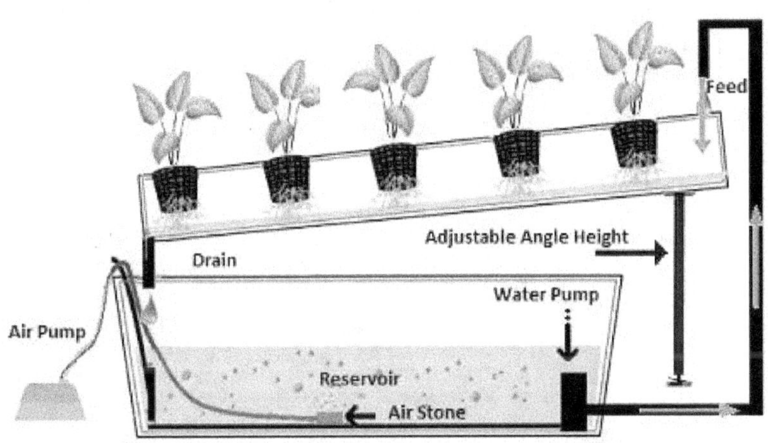

The machine may be very small but long channels are loaded with film when used in large-scale operations and the same system is simply notched up to a bigger level. Because of this system's shallow depth, it is best suited for small, fast growing crops such as lettuce and some kinds of herb. The method is very successful but with small fast growing plants of this type there is a danger that they will die quickly in the event of the drying out of the roots so there is little time to respond if there is some kind of malfunction in the system or electrical failure.

WATER CULTURE SYSTEM

The root is continuously kept moist in this system by the very delicate splashing of tiny nutrient mix droplets. Despite their roots hanging down into the pond, the plants in are suspended. Instead of a water pump an air pump is mounted in the tank and the water is aerated at a level that makes the water look like it bubbles slightly.

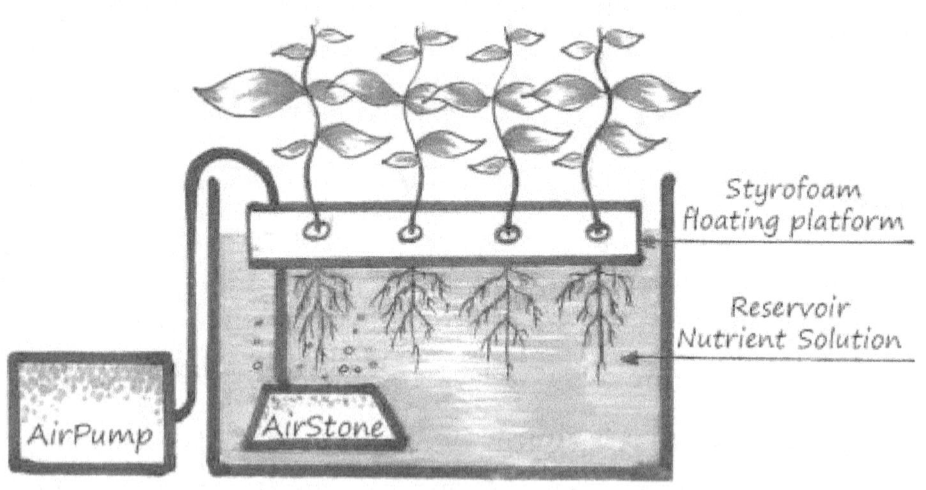

Since the top of the roots is just above the surface of the nutrient mix the pump's bubbling action can allow droplets to reach the roots. This method can be as simple as a large plastic bucket with a hole or holes cut into the lid which suspends the roots. Then the air pump is mounted in the bucket's bottom, and the lid put back on. (You may need to carve a groove into the pump for the lead).

The most challenging part of the operation is to adjust the depth of the water so that it splashes the roots correctly. Don't panic if the lower roots enter the solution so long as there's still plenty of air-exposed root content. Make sure the lid is made of a material which holds the roots in the dark.

This approach guarantees that a sufficiently well-oxygenated combination enters the roots but also includes control of the solution depth. More advanced water culture network systems are used commercially but at the same time it is just an improvement of the system used by the Aztecs which I described at the start of this book.

AEROPONICS

Another modification of the hydroponic system is called aeroponics, but as you will see the main characteristics vary very little from the other methods that you have seen. The plants are once again protected above the water supply only this time the solvent is sprayed onto the roots.

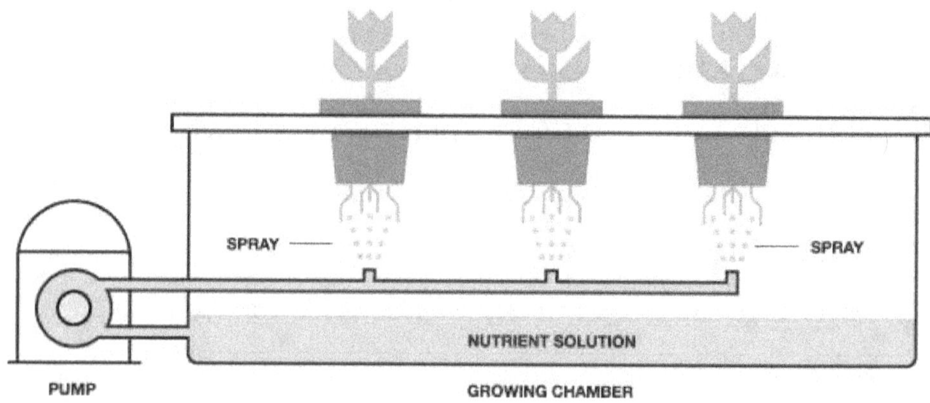

No growing medium is needed as with NFT. Think of those thin, fine sprays that you have on an ordinary irrigation system for your greenhouse. The nutrient solution is pumped from the reservoir and passes through the sprayers instead of going directly to the routes which wet the roots with a fine mist of water. Excess water can then be collected in trays and run back to the river although the spray further expands the water, making it more difficult to recapture the nutrient solution. Many industrial systems do not try to recapture the moisture but instead aim to control the distribution system in such a way that minimum waste is present.

THE WICK SYSTEM

This is by far the easiest of all the mechanisms which have been addressed so far. The plants being grown are potted in their growing medium and then placed above a fertilizer mix tank. You could have a plastic container at its most simple, with a plant inside placed on a nutrient bucket.

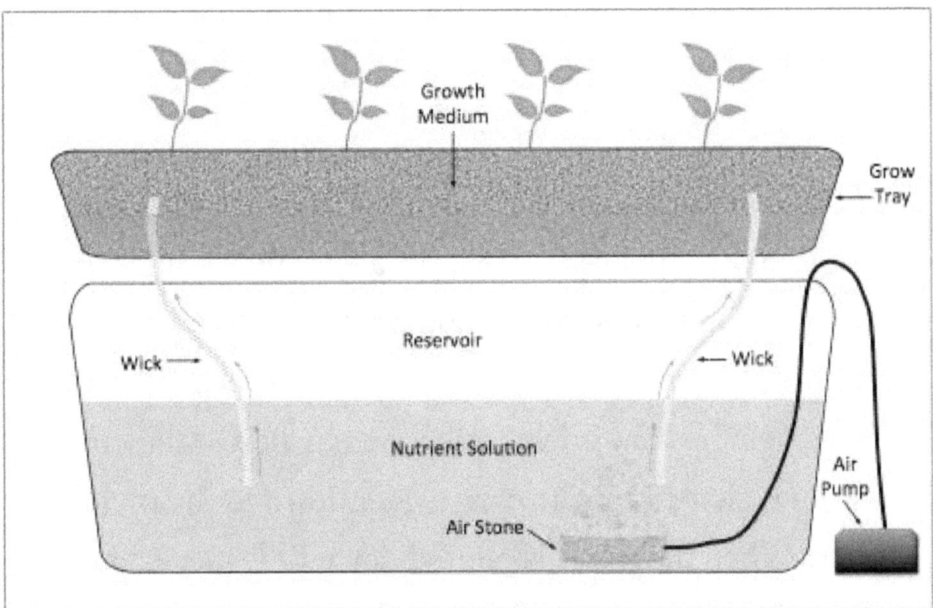

A wicking layer is then placed between the growing medium and the mixture of nutrients. This can be any substance that holds moisture like a hemp rope, underfelt carpet strips or some twisted Hessian sacking strips. There are no moving parts, there are limited material costs if any and there is very little expertise needed to put it all together.

However this approach has multiple problems. First of all, only small plants should be grown as the wick will not be able to carry enough water to meet the needs of a larger plant even if you use many. Furthermore, the wick will not uniformly distribute the nutrients and will build up those left behind in the tank to create a deposit that could become poisonous to the plant.

Thirdly, oxygenation does not occur in the river. It suggests a beginner could use this to grow a few small plants as an introduction to other hydroponic systems. It is also often used as a way for instructors to explain capillary movement, as that is what is happening here. Many may use an L-shaped tube to carry water down to the roots of a plant. When the water is poured down the pipe, capillary action in the growing medium will bring it upwards but in its true sense this isn't really hydroponic.

There is another system called aquaponics that is often confused with hydroponics which also has many parallels but is not believed to be true hydroponics. Aquaponics claims that the waste material produced by fish is used to feed plants with a method somewhat close to that of hydroponics. The application of nutrients in regulated amounts is so important to the theory behind hydroponics that it is best to consider the two topics separately.

CHAPTER 3

Different Growing Mediums

There are many different growing media that gardeners and horticulturalists all get into the habit of adapting to their own needs so we'll look at some of the most popular ones here and address their advantages and disadvantages. In all cases you are searching for a product that is light soilless that has no nutrients or contaminants that will harm the plant in any way or interact with the nutrient mix you have. It also has to be porous enough to allow quick oxygen and nutrient transport to the roots.

For two main reasons we use those inert planting newspapers. We reduce the amount of light that hits the root ball and they provide plant protection to thrive in.

The three main fabrics you're likely to encounter are typically coconut coir, perlite and LECA.

COCONUT COIR

The coconut coir is a coconut production byproduct. It is composed of the rugged outer coating that covers the coconut shell, and was used for little more than padding for inexpensive mattresses before being found as a useful product for the horticultural industry. Recognition that peat mining caused major environmental problems meant that in many instances farmers concerned with the atmosphere needed to look at new products to replace peat as a growing medium and coconut coir matched the bill. It's sold in blocks and can also be referred to as palm peat or simply coir.

When mixed with water, the blocks swell to between six and eight times their compact size so if you order any don't get too disappointed when they come and look a little smaller than you had hoped for. They are particularly good at holding moisture, and can withstand their own weight up to eight times. One of the drawbacks of this medium is that it has a propensity to be wiped about because it is so thin, and is therefore not ideal for ebb and flow processes when combined with one of the other components. After each crop growing media can be washed and reused. The mixture is rinsed in diluted bleach and then rinsed and allowed to dry again. This system can only be used three or four times for coir before it starts breaking down.

PERLITE

This is another substance which has been around for many years in the horticultural market. It is produced by heating silica flakes that expand into very small, light parts. They have strong moisture preservation and are chemically neutral and are preferred by potting mixers because it improves the capacity to retain moisture without increasing weight. When washed by bleach washing it can be used as a hydroponic planting tool several times. The light weight makes ebb and flow system difficult to use, when paired with something like LECA. It has a strong wicking motion which makes it one of the chosen wicking systems options.

LECA

LECA stands for light expanded clay aggregate and is
formed by gently heating clay particles until they spread
between six and eighteen millimeters in diameter from
anything. It is a lightweight free draining substance that is
very common in the indoor plant industry and that you
have possibly seen used in shopping centers or offices as a
mulch on potted plants. Holding moisture is fairly good but
in this respect it is not on a par with something like coir

and when high water retention is required the two products are often mixed at a ration of fifty-fifty. Then the coir retains the moisture while the LECA serves as a stabiliser to stop washing away the coir. You can get the best possible use from all items in this manner. You may choose to play with those ratios that work best for you.

These are three of the products that you are most likely to come across but there are many others that will fit well and you may want to change to either price or quality of one of the products below.

VERMICULITE

A product which looks like mica with many similarities to perlite, the mining is carried out in South Africa, India, Brazil and Zimbabwe. When mined, heating in a kiln spreads the substance and it is very light and water retentive. Like perlite, it is often used as a moisture retainer because of its neutral Ph and its light weight when mixed with potting composts. It should be used in its pure form in the hydroponic arena, and not mixed with compost or dirt.

It does not break down, and if properly cleaned, it can be used again.

PEAT BASED SOILLESS COMPOST

Peat is crazy for dried moss and plant products which have been trapped in the earth for hundreds and even thousands of years. It has been the backbone of the nursery industry for a long time, but its extensive use has resulted in a deterioration of much of the local flora and fauna in the surrounding habitats where it is mined and increasing demands for its production to be prohibited in favour of more natural items like coir. That said, it's an incredibly flexible growing medium and if you choose to use it please make sure you get it from a source that is handled sustainably.

It has outstanding retentive properties for moisture, and is very lightweight. Suppliers also pair it with biofungicides, which are naturally occurring anti-fungal agents, or natural root-stimulating mycorrhizae.

ROCK WOOL

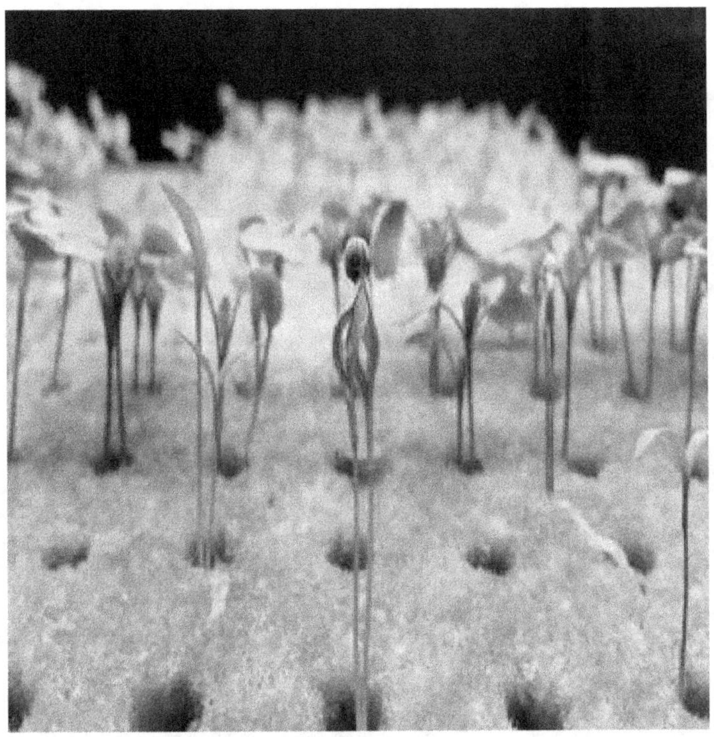

Rock wool is a flexible growing medium suitable for both ebb and flow and for constant drip systems. It holds water well and its porous nature ensures that it enables the free flow of air. It is made from a type of rock which is melted and then spun to create foam-like material. When choosing this content for your growing medium, two considerations need to be taken into account. Firstly it must be soaked overnight to ensure the Ph is stable and subsequently it does not break down and disposal can be a concern.

This lightweight foam has been used for decades by the florist industry and is suitable for hydroponic small scale producers. It can carry its own weight in water up to forty seconds, and still be breathable. It is suitable for beginning seeds as well as cuttings, making it a good tool for the basic wick method. Such properties can be used in any of the six major increasing systems and the Ph is neutral.

ADDITIONAL OPTIONS

As long as the growing medium does not contain nutrients and is safe to drain, there are plenty of items that are not connected to the horticultural industry that work well in the hydroponic world and you are free to step out of the box and play with whatever ingredients you find fit the bill can. Those light weight packing peanuts you had sitting around in the garage with no particular use for, are one example. In the early days of hydroponics the sand of Builder was commonly used. To leach out any contaminants it has to be rinsed, and it has a low water retention potential but it does work. Be vigilant however, because when it has been soaked a few times it begins to pack down and then drainage can deteriorate.

Gravel is another cheap material and is easy to find. It does not give water retention but these two qualities may sometimes prove attractive. Sawdust is often used in large-scale tomato growing in Australia, because it preserves moisture and is often natural. When you want to play with this stuff, ensure that it has not been tainted with any chemicals while still in the sawmill. They could be harmful to your crop. This appears to break down but is quickly substituted because this is typically free.

Rice hulls are bi-products of rice cultivation. Because they decompose, they are as successful as perlite, so they will have a limited lifespan. This may not be a problem as it is generally cheap or free and daily replacement is required as there continues to be an accumulation of salts that are harmful to plant growth.

CHAPTER 4

Nutrient Solutions

What hydroponics is all about is getting the correct nutrients to the base of your plant roots. The theory behind plant nutrition is quite complex and can seem quite intimidating at first but you don't need to become a plant scientist to get to grips with what you need to learn to be a good grower. Nonetheless, it will help you know some of the facts so you get an idea of what's going on and what all of those ingredients are.

There are many different nutrients a plant needs in order to thrive and they will soon die without. The three primary nutrients are called macro nutrients, although the need for a variety of other nutrients is much lower.

The three macro nutrients are: Nitrogen (N): used in the chlorophyll and amino acid production.

Phosphate (P): used in the sugar, oil, flowers and fruit processing.

Potassium (K): used in starch sugar production, roots, and general hardiness.

Such three ingredients are always more commonly listed on bottles or packets of nutrients and supplied in relative amounts to their volume and if you were to see 15:9:12 you would know their quantities were fifteen percent Nitrogen, nine percent Phosphate and twelve percent Potassium. That would make thirty-six percent of the mix with the remainder being turned over to water and micro-nutrients. It should be remembered that NPK also gives the three figures in the same order although the percentage of each will differ according to their expected use.

In hydroponics the most widely given nutrients come in a powdered or condensed liquid form that you would then dilute according to the manufacturer's instructions. To my experience the liquid method is by far the most realistic and convenient to use, and that of many other growers.

As I mentioned earlier, the reservoir should be a tank that does not require light to reduce the possibility of building up mold and algae. This tank should be at least the same size as the pots or tray it feeds and maybe bigger. Do not combine the nutrients in the tank but substitute them with water during Premixing.

Your water's pH level is very critical, because if it is either too high or too low it can have a detrimental effect on the nutrient taking up. Ideally you want between 5.5 and 7.0 this to be. Too much chlorine can also have adverse effects, so that it is necessary to deal with it too. When you stand twenty-four hours in water in a tank the chlorine breaks down. Alternatively, you can buy distilled water that seems to me to be a bit of a waste of time or you can collect rain water that will be chlorine-free and seem to me the most appropriate solution to the problem of chlorine. Don't be too disturbed by the amounts of chlorine as they don't kill plants and water that has waited twenty-four hours appears to be perfect.

The pH is most often influenced by the amount of calcium present therein. Too much calcium contributes to hard water and high pH. This will need to be measured with a pH tester and if it is outside the given range then you can apply a few drops of a chemical to increase it or another to decrease it based on the reading you receive. Most hydroponic manufacturers offer a two-part package to increase and lower pH. Just dilute a few drops of either one or the other to either boost or lower the pH to the level required. Do this blend in a little at a time and then let the water settle down before you try again. It's nice to have a general idea of your water's pH before you start first, but after that most of the pH checking should be performed after you've applied the different nutrients as they will actually change the pH values. The wireless measuring tool is quite cheap and simple to use, a little like a thermometer.

Having a second tank is one way to make your life easier. One is going to be in use and the other just going to be full of water. This will insure that the water is at the same temperature so that plants do not have to cope with a drastic change in temperature, and will also guarantee that you are free of any chlorine when using tap water from the mains. Aim to use tepid water at about 18 ° C at all times but don't make this a big issue, as you're going to have enough to get to grips with right now.

It's time to start combining the nutrients once you have your water more or less pH balanced and for the moment I'm just going to deal with purpose-bought hydroponic nutrients. These normally come in three sections which are combined for the plants you are growing according to the manufacturer's instructions. These tend to come along with a map for a variety of plants and a week-by-week dose based on the plants ' maturity. You will want to observe this map very closely in the beginning but as your level of experience grows you will no doubt begin playing with your own recipes. Nearly all hydroponic gardeners create their own recipes and start adding a set of additional products which they all swear are the best for the plants they intend to produce. I'm going to get into some of those ingredients late but we're just going to stick to combining the three-part essential nutrients for now.

Once you've got the three bottles and find the right section of the map that refers to your plants and the development point they are at you will need to put them together. Don't just throw them all in a pan and pick it up. They will react with each other in heavy concentration and produce an effect called blocking, which inhibits their individual performance. Alternatively, put a few liters of water in a bucket that's the same size as your tank. The water will need to be chlorine-free and at the right pH. That will be fine, of course, if you have the second tank already packed. Add the right amount of the first ingredient into a weighing beaker and add it into the water afterwards. Then wash the beaker out and wait the second nutrient for two minutes before repeating the process. Repeat the process eventually with the third nutrient. Remember to prevent obstruction, it is necessary to wash out the measuring beaker between nutrients. You can also buy some cheap measurement syringes and use a different one for each nutrient to prevent the risk of mixing them up.

Once I have all my nutrients in the reservoir and after adding the three I have waited for a minute or two then I give the reservoir a bit of a stir. I should retest my pH at this point to ensure the values are still within the agreed range of 5.5 to 7.0. The pH is expected to ramp up slightly over time as the plant draws up the nutrients. Because this is the case, if you could keep the pH just marginally below zero, it would be best if you could keep it to around 6.0. I then check my combination using a particular meter called a PPM meter or an EC meter and sometimes a TDC meter. Effectively all of them do the same. They calculate the nutritional content of the salts. PPM stands for parts per million, EC stands for Electrical conductivity and TDS stands for the total salts required. This simple to use little tool will often be used during the growing period as you will need to track the nutrient mix continuously to ensure that the plant gets everything it wants. Getting to grips with nutrient mixes is one of the trickiest aspects of hydroponic gardening and I don't want to make it seem so difficult because you can normally know everything you need just by watching the mixture map. Remember that each manufacturer will have a different recipe, so that each method will be slightly different.

What you're going to do with the plant changes at different times of its growth cycle, and that's why the nutrient combination needs to change. To get going you want plenty of nitrogen to get the plants to bloom as soon as possible. Later you will decrease nitrogen but raise the phosphates to improve the rooting and fruiting of the blooms and you will need small amounts of micronutrients all the way through the process you prepare. There will usually be a strong desire in the early days to add more nutrients hoping this will produce more and faster growth. In fact, for the plant too much nutrient can be worse than too little nutrient so if you have to exploit the advice of the manufacturers seek to always err on the side of less rather than more.

Now you've got the tank to the pH you want and the nutrients to the point the supplier advises you are set to start pumping. Some systems require circulation at least twice everyday and if you can get it up to once every two hours without water logging the plants that would be even better. You should use your meter every couple of days to test the nutrients. If they tend to get small then you can add a top-up blend that is essentially a mild version of the blends you use without the micro nutrients. The explanation is that plants use a lot of macro nutrients and only a very small amount of micro nutrients. When you apply more micro nutrients the environment builds up and becomes poisonous to the plants. Outdoor systems should not be subjected to heat, which will dilute the system's power.

You will change the nutrient blend completely after two weeks. It's okay to dump the old mix on any plants you have in soil garden. Wash out the tank of hot water or distilled bleach before making up the next mix. You're then ready to start a new tank, if chlorine-free water is available. This is also a good time to check the rest of the system to see if it functions and there is no trace of algae. If you are using them, pay particular attention to mist eyes, as they are quickly obscured by building up micronutrients.

While I recommended inspecting your device you should check your plants daily to make sure they are strong and healthy and show no signs of stress. Again, they'll let you know very easily if there is any system problem. When you've picked the crop then it's a good idea to strip off the entire unit and send a thorough cleaning to everything.

To Recap: By now you may begin to feel like you've been bombarded with a little too much information particularly if hydroponics is something you've never been familiar with before. The whole idea is to make sure you get a nutrient-rich solvent with an almost neutral pH at the roots of your plants. When you concentrate on those goals, you're not going to go too far off. You'll need an EC meter for the salts or nutrients and a pH meter for that. You can buy fairly cheap units that do all calculations for you so it's not hard to check the rates. You should have the mixture tested once a day. Small-scale units continue to fluctuate more than larger units, so home growers need to be as sensitive to shifts as big-scale producers.

In case pH gets too high or too low then apply a few drops after diluting of the correct drug. There are two drugs that you can use for this and they clearly state that they are either designed to raise or decrease the pH. You should not try to change the pH more than 0.5 in either way in one day as you might scare the plants. Larger shifts are impossible, because you began with the correct pH level.

The EC meter will provide you with a reading of the water conductivity, based on the amount of salts it contains. Aims for a range of 1.2 to 2.0If it goes above this you can dilute the blend by adding water and if it goes below then you can top it up as instructed by the maker.

CHAPTER 5

Plants to Grow

One of the great advantages of hydroponics is that you can cultivate a large variety of crops. The choice is infinite in many respects, but you must take into account the constraints imposed on you by the scale of your unit and the room in which it is situated. If you're a big producer in a green house set up you'll definitely want to concentrate on a small range of crops that sell quickly and if you're a home grower living in an apartment then maybe it's best to focus on just the crops you need the most.

A good starting point for the small producer is always with lettuce, as it is a salad product that is consumed everyday by ninety per cent of westerners. It is also a product that takes up little space and freshly harvested really tastes better.

Additionally, you can also pick enough leaves for a salad while allowing the plant to keep growing.

Tomatoes are the second most popular Crop. If there is one crop that automatically tastes better than all the others when harvested and consumed, then it must be the tomato.

There are hundreds of varieties so choose one you think you can love and that doesn't take up too much space. Two plants with different varieties can expand if possible, growing at different times so you can harvest for a longer period. When you pair the hydroponics with growth lights and growing indoors then you can have tomatoes practically throughout the whole year.

Another plant which can be very rewarding is the cucumbers. We go for a dwarf variety in an indoor environment and have a frame on which they can climb.

Not only are peppers easy to grow, they also make remarkably attractive plants, particularly if they are the varieties in bright colours. Another variety that we use in our homes on a regular basis for immediate savings.

Spinach is one of the most common vegetables on the vine, and is rich in vitamins and iron. There are many variations these days ranging from those with small rounded leaves to more typical plants with longer leaves. We can all have several leaves harvested thus allowing the parent plant to expand and replicate new leaves again.

Of fruit strawberries, one of the better fruits in both private and industrial settings for the hydroponic manufacturer is. With the greatly expanded growing season you'll have, there's high potential for good economic returns.

Blue berries are currently experiencing a huge increase in popularity due to their high levels of antioxidants which have proven health benefits. When growing in the field, they like an acid soil and as it is so easy to control acidity in a hydroponic production unit, this makes them good candidates for domestic and commercial production.

When you actually work out what proportions you get when you buy them in a store, herbs can be surprisingly expensive! It makes sense to grow your own and even if you only wish to grow enough for yourself and your children, you may find that you produce more than you can consume. You are extremely likely to find ready buyers among your relatives and neighbors, if you inquire around. Basil is used as an alternative to the salads in a variety of dishes. It is rich in antioxidants, as well. A very easy to grow herb, when you look at the price per kilogram it costs you a small fortune in supermarkets.

The other genuinely easy herb to cultivate is cilantro. With its many health benefits and various culinary applications, this is a reliable crop that can be grown within four weeks and can easily produce two and at times three crops per year.

CHAPTER 6

Pests and Diseases

There's one sure thing about any method of gardening and that's that at some point or other you'll still run into pest and disease problems. In the case of hydroponics the insect issue is considerably reduced because your crop does not thrive in the soil where many pests prefer to lay their eggs and hibernate. Sadly, that still doesn't mean you're going to be totally immune to receiving attention from nasty creatures as those healthy looking leaves and fruits are going to be just too much for them to ignore and find other ways to get at an easy meal.

One of the most important skills that any gardener knows is observation. Bugs and insects have developed different defense mechanisms, and the biggest one is the desire to blend in with their surroundings so that they can go unseen for as long as they can.

The technique for success is very fast breeding. When it comes to detecting bugs, the gardener almost has to develop a sixth sense. Only a healthy looking lettuce will see a casual look, but the trained eye will quickly see one or two small aphids hiding under the leaves. If they are dealt with quickly then the issue has been averted but left to their own devices within a matter of days those few aphids will multiply to almost plague proportions and then you're at risk of all harvest and getting rid of them now requires all out war.

Take the time to look carefully at your plants, turn the leaves over and use a magnifying glass if need be. Even learn to recognize when a plant doesn't look healthy at a hundred percent and even displays the slightest signs of stress.

These are some of the several common bugs you'll possibly meet. Mealy Bug An oval-shaped insect which sucks sap from leaf veins.

They create a sticky substance known as honey dew that often gives away the presence of them. These can be treated by brushing on a cotton ball with rubbing alcohol or by treating with an insecticide cleaner.

Spider mites These tiny insects are almost invisible to the naked eye and flourish in conditions of a green house. You often only become aware of them when you see a fine web surrounding the underside of leaves and when they suck out the chlorophyll the base of leaves starts to become a mottled color. Late trapped in minor infestations they can be killed easily by misting the leaves with a light soapy solution.

Thrips Tiny, winged insects a bit larger than a pin's head and like to drink sap too. Leaves are blurred and loose in color. We are best treated by pouring soapy water.

Aphids There are different types of aphids but they all have one thing in common and that is they can reproduce very easily. It is calculated that if all of the descendants from a single aphid lived for a year then their combined body weight would be enough to send the planet out of orbit. We are, luckily, very fragile creatures for us, and if you find them early we can be dealt with before we fly off to another world. They are sap suckers, and tend to favor green leaf tops. A quick blast of soapy spray renders them easily destroyed.

This is a very short list of some of the most popular pests but the ones I have identified are many more and many variations. What I have wanted to stress is that if you spot them early, they're easy to deal with. Since most of the plants you cultivate are likely to be nutritious, you need to determine if you will use pesticides or herbal methods to control your pests. Organic pest control tends to be cheaper, and since I don't want to be subjected to more toxic chemicals than I need, I prefer to choose them. Nonetheless, there's a vast array of chemical sprays and treatments on the market that are extremely effective in killing any insect you care to mention and you just have to go into a garden center and explain your concern and you'll be given a range of weapons to react with.

The repertoire is more minimal on the organic front but here are some of the therapies which Have worked perfectly well for me.

Insecticide soaps can be sprayed from a regular spray bottle, and they are my preferred weapon. Using common house hold products, you can buy them or make up your own using any amount of recettes off the net.

Neem oil is made from an evergreen tree that originates in India and is now commonly cultivated around the globe. Both the organic gardening industry and the cosmetics industry admire the gasoline. It will be available online or in most nurseries.

Tea Nettle. This is a food, which can be made by any gardener who has access to nettles. Just soak a large handful of nettles for five minutes in gently simmering water, then pipe the greenish brown liquid into a spray bottle. It becomes more effective as it grows older and is a great deterrent to insects but beware of smelling.

On the front of the disease the main threat stems from high humidity and the near planting density typical in the hydroponic system. This makes growers vulnerable to molds and mildews, of which there are many, particularly greenhouse producers. The trick is to improve airflow as much as possible and reduce humidity to the lowest acceptable levels the plants can take.

When you practice good garden hygiene, both the rodents and the disease will be minimized. Remove dead plants and leave immediately, then throw them away. Both machinery for crops and greenhouses is thoroughly cleaned and disinfected. Using devices designed for the hydroponic system so that other plants in the greenhouse do not involuntarily take in disease spores. If you use rising lights then don't be tempted to share the light with other house plants you might have because you risk spreading problems.

CONCLUSION

Hydroponics may seem a little daunting in the beginning but as you begin to work with the different systems and approaches you may find that you are starting to get a feel for the topic. This is still a fairly new approach in gardening terminology and we are all improving as the program progresses. There are some really cheap and easy approaches to play with, and once you've seen how simplistic hydroponics really is and how much greater a yield can be accomplished,

The aim is to decide whether a healthy plant will be produced using water and nutrient solution rather than soil. With no unneeded substance molecules impeding the roots of a plant, the nutrients may be consumed quicker, enabling the plant to grow faster and stronger. Because of the use of continuous fertilizer and water feeding, hydroponic plants have grown much larger and produced quicker leaves than typical soil plants.

For this cause the null hypothesis is dismissed as the evidence does not help the logic. The daily use of fertilizer throughout the day has helped the plants grow at a controlled and steady pace. The null hypothesis suggested the use of a hydroponic system would have no impact on the plant's growth and health. The null hypothesis was rejected as this was not true and the alternative hypothesis is accepted.

This experiment is aligned with another experiment which evaluated the use of various kinds of bags against soil in hydroponics. The result of this experiment was that the tomatoes grown in hydroponic bags yielded more tomatoes and thus raised more money. Interestingly, the experiment conducted with this project indicated the use of a hydroponic system would result in greater and more tasteful growth.

Hydroponic agriculture can be an ideal way to grow healthy organic food in an economic way. Start small and grow with time before making a decision, and see it for yourself. This machine is already being used to grow many of the products that we buy in the supermarket and consume on a daily basis and there's no excuse why you shouldn't be using some of that development for your own home and maybe even looking to expand to bigger things from there.